Growing Leaders in Healthcare
Lessons from the Corporate World

Brett D. Lee, PhD, FACHE, dedicates this book to his wife, Mindy, and his son, Preston, for being the support and inspiration in his life.

James W. Herring, PhD, FACHE, dedicates this book to his wife, Beverly; son, John; and grandson, Gabriel, who have encouraged him in this project.

―――――――――――――

The authors acknowledge Christopher J. Durovich, president and CEO of Children's Medical Center–Dallas, for his support and editorial contributions to this book. He continues to be a champion of positive change in the center's leadership development efforts.

Your board, staff, or clients may also benefit from this book's insight. For more information on quantity discounts, contact the Health Administration Press Marketing Manager at (312) 424-9470.

This publication is intended to provide accurate and authoritative information in regard to the subject matter covered. It is sold, or otherwise provided, with the understanding that the publisher is not engaged in rendering professional services. If professional advice or other expert assistance is required, the services of a competent professional should be sought.

The statements and opinions contained in this book are strictly those of the author(s) and do not represent the official positions of the American College of Healthcare Executives or of the Foundation of the American College of Healthcare Executives.

Library of Congress Cataloging-in-Publication Data

Lee, Brett D.
    Growing leaders in healthcare : lessons from the corporate world / Brett D. Lee and James W. Herring.
        p. cm.
    Includes bibliographical references and index.
    ISBN-13: 978-1-56793-312-3 (alk. paper)
    ISBN-10: 1-56793-312-2 (alk. paper)
    1. Health facilities—Business management. 2. Health services administrators. 3. Leadership. I. Herring, James W. II. Title.
    RA971.3.L44 2009
    362.1068—dc22   2008044988

The paper used in this publication meets the minimum requirements of American National Standard for Information Sciences—Permanence of Paper for Printed Library Materials, ANSI Z39.48-1984. ⊚™

Project manager: Jennifer Seibert; Acquisitions editor: Janet Davis; Cover designer: Anne LoCascio

Health Administration Press
A division of the Foundation of the
    American College of Healthcare Executives
1 North Franklin Street, Suite 1700
Chicago, IL 60606-3529
(312) 424-2800

Eight Lessons

MAKING THE CASE FOR STRUCTURED LEADERSHIP DEVELOPMENT IN HEALTHCARE

The concept of leadership development in healthcare has become more critical as the industry grows more complex. The days of healthcare organizations thriving under cost-based reimbursement and fee-for-service models have been replaced with multiple public and private third-party payers, increasing federal and state oversight, labor shortages and unionization, and a growing population of uninsured or underinsured consumers. The late management author Peter Drucker said, "Everything rises and falls with leadership." Today's healthcare industry has proven him correct, as leaders struggle to adapt and develop their skill sets to meet the changing demands of an increasingly challenging work environment.

The most successful companies recognized long ago that effective leadership is their only sustainable competitive advantage, and they have invested accordingly to create structured identification and development programs for emerging leaders. In 2002, the American Society of Training & Development reported that 85 percent of *Fortune* 500 companies sponsor formalized internal leadership development programs, and 65 percent of executives in those companies consider the development of a leadership talent pipeline and the implementation of formal succession planning processes two of senior leaders' highest priorities (Van Buren 2002).

Healthcare has been slow to adopt the concepts of structured leadership development and succession planning. A study commissioned by the American College of Healthcare Executives (ACHE) in 2007 on CEO succession planning found that only 21 percent of nonaffiliated ▸

hospitals in the United States had formal processes for identifying and developing internal candidates for senior leadership positions (Garman and Tyler 2007). This lack of attention could create a widespread leadership crisis in the next decade as a large cohort of senior healthcare leaders approaches retirement status.

THE DANGER IN RELYING TOO HEAVILY ON EXTERNAL RECRUITING

In the absence of qualified internal candidates, many healthcare organizations resort to recruiting leaders externally. In a 2004 ACHE report on the impact of CEO turnover in U.S. hospitals, recruitment of an external successor to the CEO position typically resulted in significant turnover of key executive staff within one year, including positions such as vice president (97 percent of cases), chief financial officer (42 percent of cases), chief medical officer (77 percent of cases), and chief operating officer (52 percent of cases). Because of this large-scale transition in leadership, many hospitals experiencing turnover at the CEO level reported the need to delay important initiatives such as strategic planning and the development of new service lines (Khaliq, Walston, and Thompson 2004). Healthcare organizations are complex and highly political environments, each with unique characteristics and challenges. Externally recruited leaders already need time to learn how to navigate a new system; delays caused by turnover impede progress even further.

In his book *Good to Great*, Jim Collins (2001) evaluated over 1,400 of the largest and most successful U.S. companies to identify an elite subset that demonstrated outstanding performance relative to their peers and sustained those results for at least 15 years. His analysis of these industry leaders revealed that the introduction of an external leader as a change agent, with a few notable exceptions, was negatively correlated with long-term, sustained success. Poor outcomes often can be attributed to the external recruit's attempts to make sweeping changes without first learning the current culture and values of the organization he or she has been invited to lead.

An effective internal leadership development and succession planning process can smooth leadership transitions and, as a result, help maintain organizational stability. Many leading companies have reported that high reliance on promotion from within socializes leaders at all levels to key corporate values and fosters a strong, coherent culture of leadership that can be sustained in times of leadership turnover.

The relatively poor progress in healthcare toward widespread, structured leadership development systems does not appear to be due to a lack of perceived value or need. During a 2002 Institute for Healthcare Improvement CEO leadership session, 97 percent of hospital CEOs in attendance reported that leadership development was critically important to achieving organizational strategic priorities. In the same session, however, 83 percent of CEOs reported that their organizations were unsuccessful at internal leadership development. Two of the most frequently cited bar-riers to establishing formal leadership development and succession planning processes were (1) the perception that a leadership development infra-structure is too labor and resource intensive to build and (2) the lack of internal competencies and knowledge needed to implement the develop-ment strategies effectively.

THE LESSONS

In this book, we present an overview of strategies of companies popularly recognized for their culture of leader-ship and history of effective leader-ship development, and highlight eight best-practice lessons (Figure Intro.1) that can be applied to healthcare organizations, regardless of size and complexity.

Figure Intro.1. Eight Leadership Development Lessons for Healthcare Organizations

Lesson 1: Establish Leadership Development as an Organizational Priority

Lesson 2: Define Desired Leadership Values and Behaviors

Lesson 3: Formally Assess Career Potential of Employees

Lesson 4: Emphasize Speed and Diversity in Leadership Development

Lesson 5: Create Structured Leadership Education and Development Programs

Lesson 6: Develop Depth Charts and Succession Plans for Key Positions

Lesson 7: Provide Formal Oversight of the Leadership Development Process

Lesson 8: Foster High-Potential Talent Streams

Note that these best practices are most effective when integrated as a set of activities and processes with high-level organizational sponsorship, rather than implemented as individual, uncoordinated strategies.

REFERENCES

Collins, J. 2001. *Good to Great: Why Some Companies Make the Leap . . . and Others Don't.* New York: HarperCollins.

Garman, A., and J. Tyler. 2007. "Succession Planning Practices & Outcomes in U.S. Hospital Systems: Final Report." [Online information; retrieved 10/13/08.] www.ache.org/PUBS/Research/succession_planning.pdf.

Institute for Healthcare Improvement. 2002. "CEO Leadership Session." Seminar presented by the Institute for Healthcare Improvement at 14th Annual National Forum on Quality Improvement in Health Care, Orlando, FL, December 9.

Khaliq, A., S. Walston, and D. Thompson. 2004. "The Impact of Hospital CEO Turnover in U.S. Hospitals: Final Report." [Online information; retrieved 10/13/08.] www.ache.org/PUBS/research/pdf/hospital_ceo_turnover_06.pdf.

Van Buren, M. E. 2002. *ASTD 2002 State of the Industry Report.* Alexandria, VA: American Society for Training & Development.

Establish Leadership Development as an Organizational Priority

WHY IS EXECUTIVE SPONSORSHIP IMPORTANT?

During his time as the chairman and CEO of PepsiCo, Roger Enrico created one of the world's leading executive development programs. His philosophy was simply that "the most important job of a leader is to make new leaders." He lived this philosophy by spending more than 100 days per year personally conducting leadership workshops for senior executives and emerging leaders, all while maintaining the helm of a multibillion-dollar corporation with over 200,000 employees. His commitment to leadership development was further demonstrated by the fact that 86 percent of executive vacancies were filled from within the organization during his long tenure (Charan, Drotter, and Noel 2001).

Executive sponsorship and visibility, as demonstrated by Enrico, are critical to successful organizational leadership development programs. Executive endorsement and participation ▶

lend credibility to leadership development activities and elevate the experiences and perceptions of those being developed. The CEO and all other senior leaders must view the future of their organization and the future of the internal leadership talent pool as inextricably linked. Healthcare CEOs are not required to follow the lead of PepsiCo and spend a full third of their time immersed in development efforts, but the success of these initiatives does require active CEO interest, involvement, and unqualified attention.

Research shows that leadership development practices at top companies are an inherent part of the organizational culture, and the expectation of systematic development of future leaders has become intertwined with the day-to-day responsibilities of running the business. A recent study conducted by Hay Group (2007) comparing the most successful global companies to their less successful peers found that 85 percent of top global companies reported leadership development as a high priority for senior management, compared to just 45 percent of other companies. According to another study, nearly 90 percent of senior leaders at high-performing companies reported spending at least 20 percent of their time on leadership development activities, whereas only 52 percent of their lower-performing peers could make the same claim (Orlando 2006). If the highest levels of the organization endorse and take an active role in leadership evaluation and development activities, the systematic growth of leaders becomes an expectation, rather than just another task that may fall by the wayside as the demands of daily work life compete for time and energy.

WHAT FORM DOES EXECUTIVE SPONSORSHIP TAKE?

The extent and methods of support provided by senior executives to leadership development initiatives vary widely, but the consistent theme in companies that have been successful in implementing these strategies is that leaders at all levels of the organization, particularly the very top, take a personal interest and ownership in making them work. The lessons we will share in this book are useless if not supported by the CEO and senior leadership, and executives must actively demonstrate their engagement to model the desired behavior for those being developed. The following points are examples of how executives can demonstrate their engagement.

- **Clearly articulate that the development of future leaders is essential to the success of the organization.** During his tenure as the CEO of General Electric (GE), Jack Welch was vocal in proclaiming that leadership development was the most critical aspect of his work. He stated, "I spend all of my time on developing people...the day we screw up the people thing, the company is over." Welch knew in some detail the planned career paths of more than 1,000 high-potential employees at GE and expected his executives to have this same intimate knowledge of the employees who worked in their areas of responsibility. He personally led group sessions in which employees of highest potential were reviewed and helped direct job assignments to facilitate these employees' professional growth (Stewart 1999). This level of commitment at the top of an organization clearly communicates to leaders at all levels that employee development should be a priority in their daily work.
- **Demand ownership and accountability for leadership development from leaders at all levels in the organization.** For leadership development to be infused into an organization's culture, it must be a clearly articulated goal for all leaders and essential to their personal growth and success. Furthermore, it must be reinforced by inclusion in the most important performance criteria used by the organization to formally measure quality of performance and, therefore, significantly influence leader compensation and advancement in the organization.
- **Serve as instructors in formal leadership education programs in the organization.** A powerful means for individuals at the top levels of an organization to demonstrate support of leadership development programs is to spend time sharing personal insights with emerging leaders. For example, all executives at GE are required to develop lessons based on their knowledge, experience, and values, and to articulate these lessons to participants in formal development sessions. Such approach requires significant executive commitment of time and effort. Such dedication lends credibility to the initiative and demonstrates its importance to those being developed (Fulmer and Bleak 2007).

- **Use organizational learning programs to enhance employee engagement.** To ensure the success of formalized organizational learning activities, senior leadership must clearly articulate the link between the business strategies for the organization and the leadership development processes. Organizational learning programs as part of formal leadership development can be used to communicate and translate corporate strategy so every employee understands his or her role in creating the desired future state. For example, Caterpillar Corporation, a producer of industrial vehicles and equipment, created its Leadership Quest program in 2004. The program challenged mid-level leaders to envision Caterpillar's corporate strategy for the next 15 years. Their recommendations were presented to the CEO, Jim Owens, and eventually became the basis for Caterpillar's strategic plan, dubbed "Vision 2020." Healthcare leaders can similarly use formal organizational learning programs to engage those with formal and informal leadership authority and build momentum toward a common vision (Vance 2008).

- **Provide formal mentoring for high-potential employees.** One of the most critical factors linked to employee commitment to an organization is employees' perception that leadership is dedicated to their continued growth and success. Senior executives can demonstrate this personal dedication by serving as professional mentors to emerging leaders. The most successful mentoring programs assign high-potential individuals to a senior executive who is typically outside of the employee's personal reporting structure (for example, a high-potential individual from the accounting department may be assigned to the chief nursing officer for mentoring). This structure allows for open communication, and the mentors' different backgrounds give the protégés a different view of the organization. Interaction typically begins in a structured, scheduled fashion and evolves into more informal, ad hoc communication.

  Much has been written about the importance of providing developmental opportunities to individuals at the appropriate "teachable moment." Employees in the midst of formal development can benefit greatly from educational experiences that occur "just in time" rather than "just in case" they need a new set of skills (Orlando 2006). The presence of a senior executive mentor at transition points in leadership development, such as an employee's promotion to a role with greater control or influence, may increase the employee's likelihood of success as he or she moves through the development process.

Although we recognize the value of formal mentoring programs, they do have significant limitations. First, competing demands for leaders' time do not permit much structured mentoring, even when they are highly committed to contribute in this manner. In addition, formally assigning high-potential employees to mentors, especially senior leaders, sends a strong message to the rest of the organization that these individuals are special. Resentment and jealousy from other employees may become an issue that must be recognized and managed.

The above list is not intended to be inclusive; it touches on only some of the ways senior leaders can provide support to formal leadership development programs. The most important lesson to remember is that regardless of the form the support assumes, a firm, clearly articulated and demonstrated commitment to internal leadership development must be present from the highest levels of the organization for the programs to be successful.

HOW CAN THE READINESS OF THE SENIOR LEADERSHIP TEAM BE ASSESSED?

Experience has shown us that executive sponsorship is a critical factor for successful organizational leadership development activities. Therefore, we suggest performing a brief assessment of the commitment and readiness of the senior team to support these philosophies before developing the programs outlined in the subsequent chapters of this book.

The questions in Figure 1.1, when discussed openly in a senior leadership team meeting, can provide insights into cultural gaps that may need to be addressed before initiating a leadership development program.

The answers to these questions may guide further discussion and reveal developmental opportunities to ensure alignment of purpose before beginning formal focus on building a leadership pipeline. All members

Figure 1.1. Senior Leadership Team Readiness Assessment

1. How much time do the CEO and members of the senior leadership team spend on the following:
   a. Discussing the development of the next generation of senior leaders?
   b. Participating in key internal leadership training and development programs?
   c. Coaching or mentoring emerging leaders or those who report to them?
   d. Working on their own professional and personal development?
   e. Meeting for the purpose of making decisions concerning key leadership development tactics, such as moving employees across organizational lines to new assignments?
   f. Apprising the board of directors of activities/progress in the area of leadership/succession planning?
2. Can the senior leadership team articulate the principles and philosophy of leadership development in the organization?

of the senior team must subscribe to the process and be personally vested in the success of the initiatives. The reservation of just one high-ranking executive is enough to cause the development programs (particularly in the early stages) to lose credibility.

REFERENCES

Charan, R., S. Drotter, and J. Noel. 2001. *The Leadership Pipeline: How to Build the Leadership-Powered Company*. San Francisco: Jossey-Bass.

Fulmer, R., and J. Bleak. 2007. *The Leadership Advantage: How the Best Companies Are Developing Their Talent to Pave the Way for Future Success*. New York: AMACOM.

Hay Group. 2007. "The War for Leaders: How to Prepare for the Battle." [Online information; retrieved 10/13/08.] www.haygroup.com/ca/register/index.asp?P = /ca/research/detail .asp?pageid = 9427.

Orlando, C. 2006. "Leadership Development Practices of Top-Performing Organizations." [Online information; retrieved 10/13/08.] www.odl.rutgers.edu/e-leadership/pdf/Orlando.pdf.

Stewart, T. A. 1999. "Who Will Run GE?" *Fortune* January 11, 26–27.

Vance, D. 2008. "Learning Practices at Caterpillar, Lyceum to Wharton CLO Program." Seminar presented to chief learning officer program at the Wharton School of the University of Pennsylvania, Philadelphia, January 20.

Define Desired Leadership Values and Behaviors

ORGANIZATIONAL VALUES

Establishment of organizational mission, vision, and values statements is common practice in healthcare. These statements inform employees, patients, and visitors why the organization exists, and what factors drive the care and services provided by the facility. These statements are typically highly visible throughout the organization, included in annual reports, reinforced during new employee orientation, and endorsed by the board of directors/trustees.

These high-level statements have tremendous value in creating a uniform organizational identity; however, because they are intended to communicate to a broad audience, they are necessarily general in nature. For example, a mission to "improve the well-being of our patients" would not be unusual. This statement expresses a noble purpose, but does little to define expectations of those in leadership roles or to guide leaders in their decision making on a day-to-day basis. ▶

In the opening to this book, we highlighted the fact that significant turnover of senior leaders is typical within one year of appointing an external candidate as CEO. With this type of wholesale change at the senior level, staff members throughout the organization often find themselves grappling with the ambiguity of the new leadership's identity, raising questions such as: What does this leadership team value? Will the organization's values change or remain the same under this new leadership? What is expected of me? What behaviors do I need to exhibit to continue to succeed? Do my values correlate with those of the new senior leadership?

To address this uncertainty and maintain continuity of purpose in times of leadership turnover, many companies create a set of core values and competencies that define their expectations of all leaders. Through time, with consistent reinforcement, these values become part of the culture of the organization and serve as the basis for leadership selection and development activities.

LEADERSHIP VALUES

Every leader has a unique personality. History has proven that individuals can demonstrate effective leadership through a wide variety of styles, as evidenced by the contrasting approaches of General George Patton, Martin Luther King Jr., and Franklin Roosevelt. Core leadership values serve as a uniform base of actions and behaviors that are expected of all leaders, and establish a cultural norm for leadership that transcends the skills, personality, or style of any one individual. A well-defined group of core leadership values can guide leaders through difficult situations or decisions and create consistency in behaviors and attitudes. This type of influence is maximized when leadership values are actively reinforced through leaders' behavior, leadership training programs, hiring/promotion consideration, and performance appraisals. A recent study of *Fortune* 100 companies revealed that over 80 percent of the respondents use explicit leadership values in employee development programming and succession planning (Orlando 2006). Examples of leadership value statements abstracted from industry are highlighted in Figure 2.1.

DEVELOPING A LEADERSHIP VALUES STATEMENT

All organizations have a set of leadership values, whether they are formally developed or not. In the absence of a structured statement of

Figure 2.1. Core Leadership Values from Industry

American Express:
Quality, customers/clients, teamwork, integrity, people

AT&T:
Thinks strategically, learns continuously, inspires a shared purpose, creates a climate for success, seizes opportunities, transforms strategy into results, builds partnerships, leverages disagreements

Federal Express:
Charismatic leadership, individual consideration, intellectual stimulation, courage, dependability, flexibility, integrity, judgment, respect for others

General Electric:
Curious, passionate, resourceful, accountable, teamwork, committed, open, energizing

Sources: American Express (2008); AT&T (2008); Cancalosi (2006); Federal Express (2008).

core values, norms are established by the leadership behaviors that are demonstrated, expected, and rewarded. For example, a skilled observer can discern whether leaders value the concept of sponsoring/ guiding continuous clinical and business process improvement and elimination of inefficiencies versus, say, accumulating more people and larger budgets (Lencioni 2002).

To change or develop desired leader behaviors, management needs to understand the current explicit or implicit leadership values, define desired future leadership behaviors, and create a plan to move leadership toward the desired state. A clearly established and communicated set of values that is expected to be demonstrated by all leaders can facilitate this transition.

Companies use a wide variety of techniques to establish their leadership value statements, but the most effective processes involve growing the statement organically through a series of discussions with leaders at all levels of the organization, typically facilitated by senior management. This interactive process increases buy-in and creates personal alignment between the values of individual leaders and the eventual, uniform expectations defined for the organization as a whole. The

Figure 2.2. Four Steps to Creating and Institutionalizing Core Leadership Value Statements

Step 1: Identify personal leadership values.

Step 2: Use personal values to create organizational core value statements.

Step 3: Assess leadership behavior against the desired future state.

Step 4: Develop strategies to move toward the identified core leadership values.

value statement development process typically occurs in four steps (Figure 2.2).

Step 1: Identify Personal Leadership Values

Initiating the creation of core leadership value statements by asking existing leaders to be introspective regarding their personal values sends a strong, positive message. The final product of this effort will be a set of formal values and behaviors that has the potential to define how leaders will be selected, developed, evaluated, and rewarded. Leaders at all levels need to emulate these values consistently in their behavior. Also important, these values should not be at odds with the personal values of the majority of those currently in leadership positions. The process of formally defining personal leadership values will allow leaders to evaluate, perhaps for the first time, the values they hold and often use (consciously

or unconsciously) as the basis for decision making. This process can be enlightening to many leaders and allows them to make more informed contributions to the creation of the organizational value statements. A form such as the one shown in Figure 2.3 can help leaders identify their values.

Step 2: Use Personal Values to Create Organizational Core Value Statements

This step requires leaders, first as individuals and then in small groups, to identify the five core values that they would like leaders to embrace. The group discussions will be informed by the personal values identified by each leader, and the strategic goals of the organization. Each group will report its five recommended values along with rationales supporting their inclusion in the final statements. A form such as the one in Figure 2.4 can assist in these group discussions.

Figure 2.3. Identifying Your Leadership Values

What values do you attempt to demonstrate as a leader (e.g., honest, driven)?	What is your personal definition of these values?	How do these values influence your leadership?
1.		
2.		
3.		
4.		
5.		

SUMMARIZING THE RESULTS OF THE DISCUSSIONS The values leaders identify from the group exercises should be summarized and ranked according to the number of times they are recommended, as demonstrated in Figure 2.5.

Values suggested most frequently and, therefore, seen as most vital to the organization's success are typically included in the final draft of the core leadership value statements.

Step 3: Assess Current Leadership Behavior Against Desired Future State

In this step, leaders critique the newly drafted core value statements and compare them to the current norms of the leadership culture. To

Figure 2.4. Identifying Core Leadership Values

What values do you believe should be espoused by all leaders in the organization?	Why should these values be included in the core value statements?	How do these values align with the strategic direction of the organization?
1.		
2.		
3.		
4.		
5.		

compile a list of potential barriers to modeling the desired values, the organization may choose to reconvene the groups that provided input into the creation of the statements. For example, a value of "delegating authority to the lowest appropriate level in the organization" may not be easy to adopt and implement if the systems, policies, or procedures of the organization do not support the concept. This process also provides a final opportunity for leaders to reconcile their personal values with those proposed for the organization before the value statements are finalized. The end product of these discussions should be a list of core leadership values with endorsement by leaders who participated in the development

Figure 2.5. Ranking of Leadership Values

Identified Values	Group																		
	A	B	C	D	E	F	G	H	I	J	K	L	M	N	O	P	Q	R	Tot
Integrity/Trust	X	X		X				X	X	X	X	X	X	X	X	X	X		13
Accountability	X	X	X	X	X	X	X	X		X			X	X	X				12
Facilitate Success of Each Other	X	X	X		X		X						X	X	X		X		9
Continuous Improvement		X		X	X		X			X	X	X						X	8
Servant Leadership					X	X	X	X		X	X				X			X	8
Effective Communication			X	X		X		X				L				X	X	X	7
Global Thinking	X	X	X							X			X	X					6
Outcome Oriented	X						X	X		X					X			X	6
Delegate Authority		X	X		X		X					X		X					6
Conviction/Inspirational				X				X											2
Focus										X		X							2
Customer Service						X										X			2

of the document, along with a gap analysis elucidating potential issues that will need to be addressed to achieve the desired future state.

Step 4: Develop Strategies to Move Toward the Identified Core Leadership Values

This final step involves the creation of strategies intended to translate the core values into day-to-day leadership behavior. Ultimately, these values should serve as the foundation for all aspects of leadership selection, assessment, and development. Strategies might include developing formal methods of behavioral interviewing or other forms of assessment that test for aptitude in the areas of defined leadership values, incorporating the core values into job descriptions and performance appraisals for all levels of leadership, using these values as the basis for the assessment of leadership potential, and informing the content of formal leadership education and development initiatives. All these initiatives can be effective in developing a sustainable, values-based culture of leadership. Each will be described in more detail in subsequent chapters.

LEADERSHIP COMPETENCY MODELS

Although explicit leadership values provide more specific information than mission statements, some institutions have found that value statements are still not sufficiently granular to guide employee development and be effectively incorporated into working documents, such as job descriptions or performance appraisal tools. For example, emerging leaders may need to know the specific set of behaviors required of them when the organization challenges them to "grow as a leader." In these instances, many companies have chosen to develop or adopt a leadership competency model that further defines the behaviors expected of leaders "living" the core values. General Electric's model, shown in Figure 2.6, is an example of value refinement (Cancalosi 2006).

Figure 2.6. General Electric's Leadership Competency Model

Core Leadership Values	Leadership Behaviors
Curious Passionate	We put imagination to work for our customers, people, and communities
Resourceful Accountable	We solve some of the world's toughest problems
Teamwork Committed	We are a performance culture that builds markets, people, and shareholder value
Open Energizing	We are a meritocracy that leads through learning, inclusiveness, and change
	Always with unyielding integrity

Source: Cancalosi (2006).

Leadership competency models can be developed internally (following a similar process as described above to create the value statements) or purchased from a variety of vendors. Expected competencies and behaviors can remain relatively general (as in the General Electric example above) or become specific, depending on the organization's preference. Internal development of a competency model has the benefit of being driven by the core values the organization has identified as important. It is, however, a labor-intensive process, particularly if the desired competency model is granular in nature and intended to be the basis of performance appraisals, professional development plans, and 360-degree leadership skills assessments.

Because of the time and effort involved, most companies have chosen to purchase the rights to an existing competency assessment tool that closely aligns with their core values. Use of an externally developed leadership competency model is advantageous because outside resources process the results of leadership competency–based 360-degree assessments, generate the corresponding reports, and contrast the results with normative data collected from other organizations that use the same competency model to assess their leaders (Gegelin et al. 2004).

A FINAL NOTE REGARDING LEADERSHIP VALUES AND COMPETENCIES

At first glance, the concept of developing leadership values and competencies can seem like an academic exercise with little practical application. We believe it is a critically important foundational step, however, to formally define what leadership should look like and establish standards to which all leaders (regardless of their position) will be held accountable. The demonstrated actions and behaviors of leaders, performance appraisal of leaders and potential leaders, reward and recognition programs, and leadership education and development can then be vehicles that drive collective understanding of these standards and turn core values and competencies into practical, day-to-day behavior.

Once core values have been identified, all leaders, especially those at senior levels, are responsible for modeling the desired behaviors. Management author Rob Lebow states, "The only thing that really changes leadership behavior is when the proclaimed values are practiced at every level, including the top." If the core values are endorsed by the highest levels of leadership and become the definition for organizational success, living them becomes an expectation rather than a suggestion (Lebow 1997). General Electric Chairman Jeff Immelt epitomized this commitment when he addressed his leadership staff in 2006: "When reviewing our core values, each of you needs to ask yourself, is this who I am today, is this the leader I have to become, or do I have to leave the company?" The result left little ambiguity about how leadership is defined at General Electric (Cancalosi 2006).

AN EXAMPLE FROM CHILDREN'S MEDICAL CENTER–DALLAS

In this book, we generally have refrained from using examples from our organization, Children's Medical Center–Dallas, an academically affiliated pediatric medical center, currently licensed for 430 beds. Like many healthcare organizations, we are learning mostly from other organizations and our own experimentation in our leadership development journey. Figure 2.7, however, shows our recently updated leadership value statements, introduced in 2008. We believe they will prove useful in articulating expected leadership behaviors at Children's.

Figure 2.7. Leadership Values

Results Leadership
- Transcendent
- Pacesetter
- Patient and Family Focused

Personal Leadership
- Respectful
- Ethical
- Courageous

Thought Leadership
- Innovative
- Global Perspective
- Participative

People Leadership
- Inspirational
- Accountable
- Empowering

(continued)

Figure 2.7. (Continued)

LEADERSHIP VALUES STATEMENT

Children's Medical Center recognizes the critical linkage between the quality and capabilities of its leadership team and the organization's continued growth and success. Accordingly, Children's will build and maintain an outstanding leadership team comprised of individuals who embrace our mission, guiding principles and a shared vision of preeminence in children's healthcare.

Members of Children's leadership team will:

Results Leadership
- Expect and inspire high performance at all levels of the organization; support systems and processes that encourage high performance
- Manage all resources in a manner that supports Children's mission and vision of preeminence
- Drive for results; set the pace for staff to follow
- Support decision-making and problem-solving at the level in the organization that is the most appropriate
- Rely on customer feedback as the key measure of quality of service results

Personal Leadership
- Display high character and integrity in all interactions; behave in an ethical, honest, trustworthy and respectful manner at all times
- Display courage in persuading others to address opportunities and problems
- Value how results are achieved; monitor the impact of one's leadership style on others and make adjustments as needed
- Foster the concept that true leaders gain authority based on their actions, not formal position
- Demonstrate an appropriate balance between work and other life activities

Thought Leadership
- Look for new and more effective ways of performing work and challenge others to do the same
- Engage in global thinking when making decisions; test whether decisions made at department or division level have a positive impact on the overall organization; base local decisions on sound information about Children's strategic goals and objectives
- Include staff in efforts that will impact their work environment

People Leadership
- Accept accountability for personal actions and for those within one's area of responsibility; encourage others to own the results of their actions and learn from sub-optimal outcomes
- Communicate effectively with people inside and outside the organization and insist upon the same from others
- Empower others to assume leadership roles whether or not they are formally designated as leaders
- Value the diversity of employees, physicians and patients; encourage employees to realize their full potential and maximize their contributions to Children's
- Engage in career and succession planning; promote from within Children's as a preferred strategy

Source: Children's Medical Center–Dallas. Used with permission.

REFERENCES

American Express. 2008. "Our Values." [Online information; retrieved 10/13/08.] http://home3 .americanexpress.com/corp/OS/values.asp.

AT&T. 2008. "AT&T Citizenship and Sustainability Report 2007/2008: Connecting for a Sustainable Future." [Online information; retrieved 10/13/08.] http://att.centralcast.net/ csrbrochure08/default.aspx.

Cancalosi, B. 2006. "GE Healthcare Best Practices: How to Become a Growth Leader." Internal training publication for GE healthcare employees, General Electric Company Press, Milwaukee, WI.

Federal Express. 2008. "Corporate Identity Quick Reference Guide." [Online information; retrieved 10/13/08.] www.fedexidentity.com/guidelines/FedEx_guidelines.pdf.

Gegelin, S. H., K. J. Nelson-Neuhaus, C. J. Skube, D. G. Lee, L. A. Stevens, L. W. Hellervik, and B. L. Davis. 2004. *Successful Manager's Handbook: Develop Yourself, Coach Others*, 7th edition. Minneapolis: Personnel Decisions International.

Lebow, R. 1997. *A Journey into the Heroic Environment: A Personal Guide for Creating a Work Environment Built on Shared Values*. Roseville, CA: Prima Publishing.

Lencioni, P. 2002. "Make Your Values Mean Something." *Harvard Business Review* 80 (10): 113–17.

Orlando, C. 2006. "Leadership Development Practices of Top-Performing Organizations." [Online information; retrieved 10/13/08.] www.odl.rutgers.edu/e-leadership/pdf/Orlando.pdf.

Formally Assess
Career Potential
of Employees

WHY ASSESS CAREER POTENTIAL OF EMPLOYEES?

Are leaders born or made? One of the premises of this book is our answer to the age-old question: a little of both. Some people seem to have more innate potential to lead than others, but we believe leaders can and should be developed. Individuals with the appropriate drive and potential can develop their abilities through experiences and education that facilitate and accelerate their advancement to leadership roles, while receiving encouragement, support, and rewards for taking advantage of such opportunities.

Another key premise of this book is that organizations play a critical role in optimizing employee development, especially individuals destined for senior-level roles. Only through leaders' concerted efforts and partnership with these employees can effective and accelerated individual development occur on a broad basis. Organizations that leave professional ▶

development to the employee alone are missing the boat by a wide margin; reliance on "natural organizational or environmental forces" stalls progress and usually results in improper development. For example, internal job posting systems, through which employees apply for open positions, do not promote effective employee development. Job posting systems do have some advantages, but when used without structured leadership development programs, they usually do not foster leadership development; when unassisted, employees have insufficient control of factors affecting their careers to produce anything close to an ideal career path for themselves.

Career potential should be assessed formally for the following reasons.

- The use of sound procedures adequately controls the subjectivity inherent in assessment of career potential.
- Assessments of career potential inform the pace of an employee's development program. For example, if an employee has the potential to achieve a position three levels above his current level, that employee's program needs to be accelerated so that the organization has enough time to reap a significant return on the investment of developing this individual. Conversely, if the employee is assessed as having no career potential beyond his current position level, development plans still need to be created, but their urgency and focus are different. Organizations need to ensure that the most significant developmental opportunities are provided to employees of highest potential, because in any hierarchical organization, such opportunities are limited.

- Organizations reap enormous psychological benefits in terms of increased morale and commitment when employees know their careers are important to leadership and that management is paying significant attention to career planning, including formalized assessment of leadership potential and other processes outlined in this book. Each employee wants to know that his or her development matters. Employees gain a sense of confidence and security when they know the organization is fostering long-term stability through the systematic identification and development of future leaders.

- Formalization of processes and functions, including systematic oversight by senior leadership, ensures that they are carried out consistently in the intended manner across the organization.
- Leadership's credibility is strengthened when employees witness the development and promotion of the most qualified individuals.

HOW FORMAL SHOULD CAREER POTENTIAL ASSESSMENT BE?

Companies that have mature career development processes assess career potential as formally as they assess performance. They record career potential estimates in secure employee records, just like performance appraisal results.

WHO SHOULD ASSESS CAREER POTENTIAL?

Many frontline managers, who typically perform most appraisals of day-to-day work performance, do not have the perspective necessary to envision or recognize performance desired at much higher leadership levels. Therefore, immediate supervisors should initiate assessments of

career potential, but the involvement of leaders at higher levels of the organization can help supervisors gain consensus and generate accurate evaluations.

Each employee (particularly high-potential employees) should be assigned to a senior leader for career assessment and development purposes—that is, each employee's career should be "owned" by an individual in senior leadership. The person best suited for the job is not always obvious, as in the case of a business analyst working in a nursing unit. One might assume that the head of the nursing unit would be responsible for career assessment and planning, but the senior leader of the finance department might be a better choice because he or she could give the employee rotational assignments related to the analyst role.

WHICH EMPLOYEE GROUPS SHOULD BE ASSESSED?

Ideally, leadership should assess the career potential of all employees and communicate that the development of each employee is important. Limiting the assessment process to certain employee groups conveys that some employees are more important than others. From a practical standpoint, however, an organization may choose to start the implementation of career assessments at higher management levels (for example, evaluation of those in senior or middle management positions) to introduce the concepts. These leaders can then be instrumental in cascading the assessment process down the ranks.

HOW OFTEN SHOULD CAREER POTENTIAL BE ASSESSED?

Career potential typically is assessed on an annual basis, similar to the performance appraisal process. Currently there is no consensus regarding when the career potential process should be conducted. Some organizations see efficiency in completing career development and performance assessments at the same time. We believe there is some advantage, especially to an organization that is beginning the career potential assessment process, to conduct the assessment at a different time. This separation may help leadership distinguish the different criteria and thought processes neces-

sary to make valid career potential estimates.

WHAT FORM SHOULD CAREER POTENTIAL ESTIMATES TAKE?

We have observed three main methods of assessment: by position/job level, by pay grade level, and by number of positions/job levels above the employee's current level.

If the assessment is based on position or job level, it should accurately reflect the organization's hierarchy (e.g., job titles). This approach can be used for assessment of potential in managerial or professional career paths, as well as continued potential for advancement in nonmanagement roles. An example assessment form for employees in a hospital's human resources department is shown in Figure 3.1.

If the assessment is based on pay level (sometimes referred to as *pay grade*, *position classification level*, or *job valuation point range*), the organization's designations are used. Use of pay level is advantageous in that it typically reflects increasing position scope in an orderly fashion; higher pay grades usually reflect positions of greater authority. The main

Figure 3.1. Employee Career Potential Assessment Form

Employee: _____

Current Job Title: _____ **Current Pay Grade:** _____

Potential: Highest level in the organization you believe this employee has the potential to reach (Select only 1 box of the 12 boxes below.)

Management Ladder

❏ Executive

❏ Senior Director

❏ Director

❏ Manager

❏ Supervisor

Exempt Ladder

❏ Senior Staff HR Consultant

❏ Senior HR Consultant/Recruiter/Analyst/Specialist

❏ Staff HR Consultant/Recruiter/Analyst/Specialist

❏ HR Consultant/Recruiter/Analyst/Specialist

Nonexempt Ladder

❏ Senior HR Associate

❏ HR Associate

❏ HR Assistant

Readiness: When might the employee be ready for the above level?

❏ Ready now   ❏ 1–12 months   ❏ 1–3 years   ❏ 3–5 years   ❏ >5 years

Developmental Experiences Needed: Include rotational or promotional assignments. (Note: These experiences should become part of the employee's development plan.)

Supervisor/Manager Name: _____ **Date:** _____

Reviewed By: _____

disadvantage is that pay range gradation is not always clearly understood by supervisors at all levels in the organization.

If the assessment is based on the number of position/job levels above the employee's current level, the assessment is typically recorded as follows:

- No potential beyond current level (0)
- 1 position/job level of potential (1)
- 2 position/job levels of potential (2)
- 3+ position/job levels of potential (3+)

A modified version of the example form in Figure 3.1 can be used for assessment based on any of these methods.

ON WHAT BASIS SHOULD THE CAREER POTENTIAL ASSESSMENT BE MADE?

Another premise of this book is that all employees, whether or not they occupy formal leadership positions, have the potential to be leaders and show leadership behaviors. If this supposition is true, the leadership values, competencies, and behaviors discussed in Lesson 2 are criteria we can use to assess leadership potential. In early career stages, these behaviors are harder to detect and future leadership performance at much higher organizational levels is difficult to predict. For this reason, organizations that have mature assessment processes teach their leaders to be conservative in projecting career success. For example, a new employee's estimate may reflect only two or three levels above his or her current assignment until management observes a few years of his or her performance. Also, until an employee has supervisory experience, most organizations are reluctant to project high leadership potential.

HOW RELIABLE ARE SUBJECTIVE CAREER POTENTIAL ASSESSMENTS?

Organizations that routinely assess career potential report that, with increasing experience and practice, the annual process gets easier and leaders making the assessments show greater consensus. Critics might assert that the process becomes smoother because leaders simply review the prior years' assessments and do not look diligently for significant changes in career potential over time. Most organizations, however, would disagree and attribute the improvement to knowledge acquired over time. Years of observation provide leaders with a rich basis of behavior to assess, and through experience, leaders acquire a better understanding of organizational leadership values and competencies.

SHOULD EMPLOYEES BE TOLD THEIR CAREER POTENTIAL ESTIMATE?

Even though the concepts of openness, joint ownership of development plans, and transparency are appealing and popular with almost everyone, organizations have learned that communicating each year's career potential estimate to employees can have negative consequences for the following reasons.

■ High-potential employees feel good about their status, but their motivation often wanes as a result of the belief that they "have it made" and do not have to strive as hard to maintain the status.

■ Career potential estimates may change in either direction over time. A downward change may be short lived, lasting no more than a year or two. If the employee becomes aware of the regression, he or she may become too discouraged to continue the development process.

■ Organizations that (unwisely, in our opinion) maintain and disclose a list of high-potential employees create a caste system among employees that defines "haves" and "have nots," causing resentment and interfering with collaboration.

High-potential employees should be provided positive reinforcement during their regular performance reviews so that they remain mindful of their importance to the organization, but to avoid the consequences above, formal career potential estimates should be kept confidential and appropriate steps should be taken to maintain data security. Many human resources information systems are not sufficiently sophisticated to ensure confidentiality. Existing systems may need to be enhanced, or a separate, high-confidentiality record storage system may need to be developed.

RECOMMENDED READING

Charan, R., S. Drotter, and J. Noel. 2001. *The Leadership Pipeline: How to Build the Leadership-Powered Company*. San Francisco: Jossey-Bass.

McCall, Jr., M. W. 1998. *High Flyers: Developing the Next Generation of Leaders*. Boston: Harvard Business School Press.

McCall, Jr., M. W., J. Mahoney, and G. M. Spreitzer. 1995. "Identifying Leadership Potential in Future International Executives." In *In Charge of Change: Insights into Next-Generation Organizations*, edited by D. Ready. Lexington, MA: International Consortium for Executive Development Research.

Smith, A., and R. Rogers. 2003. "White Paper—A Blueprint for Leadership Success." [Online information; retrieved 10/14/08.] www.osp.state.nc.us/ewl/documents/Ldwp07_LeadershipBlueprintWP.pdf.

Emphasize Speed and Diversity in Leadership Development

WHY SPEED COUNTS IN LEADERSHIP DEVELOPMENT

In the introductory chapter to this book, we referenced the growing complexity of the health-care industry. For example, consider the education, background, and experience desired of a CEO of a sizable healthcare system in the United States today. The list of qualifications is long. To be considered competent, a CEO is expected to possess understanding and appreciation of the following key functions:

- Inpatient services, including general medical and surgical units; intensive care unit operations; perioperative services; and various specialized services, such as transplantation and patient transportation ▶

- Outpatient services, including hospital-based physician practices, and emergency services
- Ancillary services, including radiology, pharmacy, laboratory, physical medicine, respiratory care, and volunteer services
- Family support services, such as social work, pastoral care, and translation services
- Primary care services and their impact on the demand for inpatient and subspecialty services
- Quality functions and appropriate metrics, activities, and benchmarks to ensure the safety and efficiency of care provided
- Standards and political considerations associated with regulatory agencies such as The Joint Commission and Centers for Medicare & Medicaid Services
- Long-range business planning
- Facilities construction and management
- Financial functions, including the revenue cycle, accounting, finance, and the treasury
- Information technology
- Public and governmental affairs
- Fundraising and community affairs
- Human resources, including labor laws and union politics
- Executive compensation and benefits

- Academic and other affiliations that may affect hospital operations
- Physician relations and recruitment
- Market research and business development
- Compliance and legal issues
- Governance/board affairs
- Special functions that exist upstream and downstream of inpatient services, such as hospice, sub-acute facilities, and home health services

The list does not end there. How does a potential CEO hope to master even a portion of these diverse and imposing functions? How many work assignments would be necessary to gain cursory, much less in-depth, exposure to most or all operations crucial to the success of a CEO?

The planned career paths of potential CEOs of large, complex companies often include more formal assignments than one might expect over a span of many years to expose the candidate to essential parts of the business and to prepare him or her to comprehend the broad range of issues a CEO must manage. At Dow Chemical, for example, employees of highest potential are expected to work 10–15 rotational assignments, of 12–18 months each, in rapid succession to develop the general management and leadership skills required to assume the highest positions of leadership. Companies like Dow have learned that this rapid development will not happen without careful planning, senior leadership's dedication to plan implementation, and talented, motivated individuals who will benefit from the development opportunities (Conger and Fulmer 2003; Dow Chemical 2008).

Speed of leadership development is crucial for those slated to be CEOs. The average age of individuals assuming the role of country president (individual responsible for company operations in 1 of 60 countries) at Dow Chemical ranges from the middle 30s to early 40s. The only way to move these high-potential leaders rapidly through the requisite rotational experiences is through thoughtful planning and organization-wide endorsement (Conger and Fulmer 2003). Speed of development is important as a general principle, applicable not only to high-potential employees, but to as many employees as possible organization-wide, so that all employees, regardless of their position in the hierarchy, remain engaged and have an opportunity to maximize their contributions to the organization.

WHY DIVERSITY OF EXPERIENCE COUNTS IN LEADERSHIP DEVELOPMENT

When Robert Goizueta, the immensely popular CEO of the Coca-Cola Company, passed away in 1997, company insiders had little doubt as to who his successor would be. For several years, Mr. Goizueta had been grooming his longtime chief financial officer, M. Douglas Ivester, for the top job and had been deliberate in touting Ivester as the "heir apparent" to the CEO position. As expected, Ivester was tapped to succeed Goizueta, but just over two years later, he was forced to resign after a series of poor leadership decisions caused the value of company stock to drop significantly (Conger and Fulmer 2003).

What would cause a talented individual like Ivester to fail so quickly in a job for which he had supposedly been groomed? The answer lies in insufficiently diverse career paths, which reward individuals for excellence in a particular management skill area without providing broader developmental opportunities to master the general competencies that may be required as one assumes positions of increasing responsibility.

Ivester's brilliance and expertise in the world of finance remained unquestioned; lack of attention to gaps in his skill set (e.g., public affairs and operations management) proved to be his downfall as he moved into the broader role.

A diverse development experience is an important general principle, applicable to a broad range of employees (e.g., those being developed to lead functions such as operations, finance, information technology, facilities management, planning/operations support, public affairs, and human resources), not just those being groomed for the highest level. In our view, rapid, diverse experience separates the masters from the dilettantes in the game of leadership development.

WHAT ARE THE MAIN DEVELOPMENT METHODS?

What tools can help accelerate and diversify employee development?

- Life experiences before working with current employer
- Self-study (e.g., books, articles, distance learning through computer-based learning systems)
- Mentoring by trusted individuals at work
- Mentoring by outside coach
- Formal secondary and college education (generally obtained through pursuit of diplomas and degrees)
- Preparation for licensure/certification granted by professional organizations
- Classroom training at work or through other venues, such as executive training programs sponsored by universities
- Community and other leadership experiences outside the workplace
- Assignment to special projects at work
- Assignment to interim roles at work
- Assignment to new positions of responsibility at work

This list is not comprehensive. According to Morgan McCall, professor of management and organization, Marshall School, University of California (1998), formal didactic training can assist in development, but by far the most effective vehicles for rapid personal and professional growth are challenging work experiences. Therefore, the methods toward the end of the list are the most important to consider when contemplating an accelerated and diverse development path for all employees, especially those with high potential.

Figure 4.1. Employee Development Planning Steps

1. Formal employee development discussion with direct supervisor
   A. Completion of self-assessment and development worksheet
   B. Employee development meeting
2. Preparation of an employee development action plan
3. Review of employee development action plans by higher leadership
4. Communication of development plan elements with employees

EMPLOYEE DEVELOPMENT PLANNING

How does an organization plan development activities for employees, high potential and otherwise? We recommend the procedures in Figure 4.1, although many variations on the theme exist, depending on an organization's size and complexity and the maturity of its employee development process. Unless otherwise indicated, these procedures are designed to be implemented on an annual basis. Most employers expect this process to occur around the same time for all employees (e.g., during the third quarter). For best results, these steps should be implemented separately from performance appraisal and pay increase processes.

1. Formal Employee Development Discussion with Direct Supervisor

The purpose of the first step in the development planning process is to provide an opportunity for the employee to discuss his or her ideas and complete a self-assessment.

A. Completion of Self-Assessment and Development Worksheet

In preparation for the development discussion with his or her direct supervisor, the employee should complete a self-assessment of personal development needs and goals. Some organizations provide a form/worksheet or supplemental reading to guide the employee (examples of suggested texts are included in the reference section at the end of this chapter). Whatever form is used, the employee should be encouraged to focus on the following issues/topics:

- Personal strengths (characteristics, knowledge, skills, competencies, and abilities)
- Growth opportunities (gaps between current and desired characteristics, knowledge, skills, competencies, and abilities)
- Specific ideas about how to reduce or eliminate identified gaps in an appropriate manner and over a reasonable time frame
- Degree of time and energy employee is willing to invest to reduce the gaps
- Employee's willingness/desire to transfer to another position, if offered
- Employee's willingness/desire to accept a special work assignment within the context of the current position, if offered
- Employee's willingness/desire to accept a special training assignment within the context of the current position, if offered
- Employee's willingness/desire to be transferred to another location (if the organization has multiple locations), including willingness to move to a new residence

B. Employee Development Meeting

The development discussion involving the employee and his or her di-

rect supervisor should be scheduled for at least an hour. The supervisor listens for most of this time to gather the employee's detailed input, and offers encouragement and support. The role of the supervisor in this session is primarily to manage the discussion. By taking notes and asking clarifying questions, the supervisor ensures that the conversation covers all the points listed above.

This discussion is an important part of the development process because the employee's perceptions, engagement, motivation, and commitment are crucial to the success of a development plan. A well-conducted discussion between the employee and his or her direct supervisor should provide helpful insight into these elements.

2. Preparation of an Employee Development Action Plan

The purpose of the second step in the development planning process is to create an initial draft of an employee development action plan. Using a one- or two-page form, the immediate supervisor summarizes the discussion in step 1, including the employee's input and the supervisor's judgments concerning pertinent issues related to employee development. The following topics are essential to this summary.

- **Interests/aspirations**—An employee may choose not to pursue career advancement in terms of organizational level and, instead, stay at his or her current career level/assignment. However, a plan to remain at the same level of performance and leadership should not be acceptable (even if the employee is not assigned to a formal, leadership/supervisory position). Individual development (increasing skills and contribution) should be required of every individual in the organization. Therefore, the employee's expressed interests and aspirations should reflect his or her commitment to continuing professional/technical/leadership development.
- **Mobility potential**—If relocation is a relevant factor (i.e., the organization has multiple locations in different geographic areas), the employee's personal geographic mobility preferences should be recorded.
- **Developmental gaps**—Key developmental gaps should be defined to provide a background and basis for specific development plans.
- **Development plans**—Short- and long-range development plans

should be listed to address the gaps. Language in this section should be as precise as possible and include specific plans (including specific rotational work assignments), proposed timing, and formal assignment of lead responsibility for ensuring the plan's implementation.

Optional topics might include a summary of career history (a record of past assignments at current and past employers) and a record of strengths/competencies already developed.

The immediate supervisor should seek the employee's editorial input and concurrence on the content of this initial individual development plan. The employee should understand that elements of the initial plan that require action by others in the organization are to be negotiated and pursued at higher levels of review.

An example of a professional development plan form including key focus areas is shown in Figure 4.2.

3. Review of Employee Development Action Plans by Higher Leadership

The purpose of the third step in the process is to involve higher leadership in decision making,

Figure 4.2. Professional Development Plan

Name: _____ Date: _____

Career History:

_____
_____
_____

Interests/Aspirations:

_____
_____
_____

Strengths:

_____
_____
_____

Growth/Developmental Areas:

_____
_____
_____

Developmental Plans:

What	When	Responsible

where appropriate. For example, developmental activities such as rotational assignments and special projects may require the direction of a variety of higher leaders, including those from other organizational units to which the employee may be transferred.

The employee's immediate supervisor is responsible for conferring with his or her own supervisor to develop a course of action to test the degree of consensus on proposed elements of the plan that require decision/action by leaders above the employee's immediate supervisor. Also, as will be outlined in detail in a later chapter of this book, an oversight group should meet and decide on whether, how, and when the proposed plan element(s) should be implemented.

4. Communication of Development Plan Elements with Employees

The employee's immediate supervisor is responsible for finalizing the employee's development plan. If applicable, the input of higher leadership should be considered in drafting the final plan. The immediate supervisor should omit any sensitive element, such as a tentative plan to promote or transfer the individual

to another position, that might not materialize during the envisioned time frame.

The immediate supervisor then communicates and provides a copy of the final plan to the employee. Supervisors should be as encouraging as possible and make themselves available to discuss issues or questions that may arise as the plan is put into action.

Employees should understand that completion/implementation of all plan elements does not automatically result in a promotion, a transfer to another assignment, participation in a special training activity/course, or other advancements. Instead, employees' assignments should be individually tailored to address perceived gaps in their skill sets and to help them meet their stated career aspirations.

BENEFITS OF A LEADERSHIP DEVELOPMENT PROCESS

The costs of implementing processes such as those described in this chapter are significant in terms of time and effort; however, a number of important advantages can be realized. The following are a few of the more noteworthy benefits.

- Organizational productivity and overall performance will likely increase because the "gap reduction" methodology used to determine the content and timing of employee development plans will result in faster and more diverse development than alternative or informal approaches would foster. Employees who are more effectively developed will likely perform at higher levels.

- Employee commitment to the organization is likely to increase because the organization will have shown employees that it cares about their personal development by implementing a process that requires an individual development plan for each employee (updated annually), no matter what level or position.

- Extensive involvement of leaders, including the immediate supervisor, promotes shared ownership of the development process. Faster and more diverse development results because the employee is not required to "own" the entire process, and the most effective development methods (e.g., job rotation and assignment to special projects) are more likely to be implemented.

- Standardizing the process across the organization (as we strongly recommend) results in more efficiency and communicates to employees a more compelling and motivating story about how development is accomplished.

REFERENCES

Conger, J. A., and R. Fulmer. 2003. "Developing Your Leadership Pipeline." *Harvard Business Review* 81 (12): 76–84.

Dow Chemical. 2008. "Careers at Dow: Career Programs/Opportunities." [Online information; retrieved 10/14/08.] www.dow.com/careers/programs/index.htm.

McCall Jr., M. W. 1998. *High Flyers: Developing the Next Generation of Leaders*. Boston: Harvard Business School Press.

RECOMMENDED READING

Waldroop, J., and T. Butler. 2007. *Managing Your Career: A Module in the Harvard Business School Press ManageMentor Program*. Boston: Harvard Business School Press.

———. 2000. *Maximum Success: Changing the 12 Behavior Patterns That Keep You from Getting Ahead*. New York: Doubleday Business.

Create Structured Leadership Education and Development Programs

ORGANIZATIONAL LEARNING IN CORPORATE AMERICA

The dawn of the twenty-first century ushered in a new and interesting dynamic that has helped to reshape the landscape of global industry. Companies were faced with an increasingly competitive business climate, and many reached the same conclusion: Growth through mergers, acquisitions, or investment in new technologies provides finite returns. The leadership of these organizations came to believe that, ultimately, the skills and talents of employees are the only sustainable competitive advantage. As this epiphany became widely accepted, the most successful companies began investing heavily in the development of internal education programs. In fact, the average *Fortune* 1000 company now spends 2.5 percent of its annual operating budget on employee education and training programs (Fulmer and Bleak 2007). Such programs have given rise to "corporate univer- ▶

sities" and new senior leadership positions with a primary focus on organizational learning, such as chief learning officer.

Science Applications International Corporation (SAIC), a prominent research and engineering firm, has created an educational infrastructure with significant breadth and depth. SAIC has flourished in the first decade of this century through rapid growth of information technology (IT) outsourcing and consulting services. Because the ongoing success of these service lines depends significantly on the intellectual capital of SAIC's employees, leadership made a strategic decision to provide management and IT skills training for all staff. The company created a chief learning officer position and challenged the incumbent to launch a corporate university, called SAIC University. The university started by offering programs to grow the skills of managers and frontline engineers. It now offers an on-site MBA program through a partnership with an accredited college. Also offered are in-house programs that provide leadership development, technical training, and project management skills training for the organization's formal and informal leaders (Field 2004).

ORGANIZATIONAL LEARNING IN HEALTHCARE

The healthcare industry has been slower to invest in in-house educational program development, relying more heavily on formal degree programs that have traditionally prepared individuals for clinical professions. This dynamic is beginning to change, however, as competition for increasingly scarce clinical and leadership talent becomes more pronounced. Investment in formal, robust employee development programs such as those offered by SAIC has become the norm, and companies that do not have comparable programs have found themselves at a significant disadvantage in recruiting and retaining talented individuals. With a multitude of employment choices available to healthcare professionals, an organizational focus on continuing education, structured career growth paths, and employee development are becoming requirements rather than luxuries. If an organization does not have a clear imperative focused on helping employees achieve their desired career potential, it will fail to attract the most talented individuals. These individuals will seek opportunities with employers that do have a program in place.

WHAT STRUCTURE SHOULD FORMAL ORGANIZATIONAL LEARNING INITIATIVES TAKE?

Although a strategic focus on developing formal educational programs has become a survival skill in the competitive world of modern healthcare, organizations need not go to the extreme of developing a corporate university to be successful. There are many stops along the continuum between the absence of in-house training and a full-fledged, centralized learning function. Whether the facility houses a structured leadership academy or offers stand-alone courses, we suggest including the following key components to ensure

successful in-house training and education (see Figure 5.1).

- **Curricula driven by organizational strategy and based on desired leadership competencies:** Leadership development programs, whether designed internally or in conjunction with an outside partner (such as a consulting firm or university), provide the greatest value when the program content is linked directly to organization-specific business imperatives. For example, if a healthcare organization has a goal of improving patient satisfaction over the coming years, an internal leadership development program may include curricula designed to improve leaders' customer service skills, which may translate to improved patient satisfaction (e.g., leadership rounding, communication training, and

Figure 5.1. Key Components of In-House Leadership Development Programs

- Curricula driven by organizational strategy and based on desired leadership competencies
- Focus on leadership at all levels
- Comprehensive and diverse instructional approaches
- Executive sponsorship and active involvement

dispute resolution). Progressive organizations evaluate their strategic plans annually to determine which goals could be advanced by providing in-house education, and then use the outcomes of these discussions to develop future curricula.

Another advantage of developing an in-house educational program is that an organization can tailor its course content to its desired leadership competencies and then use those competencies to create a culture of leadership. Identified competencies should be evaluated to determine which are core (i.e., those already widely understood and practiced by leaders in the organization) and which are desired (those not widely practiced but critical to the organization's future success). Preferably, education provided through in-house development programs should be based primarily on competencies that most leaders have not yet mastered; reinforcing the same skills in perpetuity creates a recipe for obsolescence.

- **Focus on leadership at all levels:** An effective leadership development program is not focused on fine-tuning the skills of only the senior executive team or middle managers of highest potential. The primary objective of an in-house educational program should be to build a well-prepared team of leaders at all levels. Every level of leadership needs to be adequately prepared and trained. Organizations should identify key leadership groups, including prospective supervisors (those with leadership potential), frontline supervisors, middle managers, and higher-level (including executive) leadership, and customize curricula to meet the needs of each subset.

At Shell Oil, for example, three audiences are targeted: line managers, who participate in "Shell Life," a program focused on basic training in coaching, change management, delegation, and staff development; functional managers, who participate in a program that focuses on business leadership, advanced management skills, and strategic planning; and executive leaders, who participate in training that focuses on global business issues, designed to prepare individuals for the challenges of running a large, multinational corporation.

Note that as a leader assumes positions of greater authority, the focus of in-house training and development shifts from providing technical competencies to developing a generalist skill set required to critically evaluate and address broadscale issues (Shell Oil 2008).

- **Comprehensive and diverse instructional approaches:** The cornerstone of corporate education and training programs historically has been instructor-led, classroom experiences. Although these types of activities are still a critical component of a comprehensive in-house program, advances in technology have created a host of other effective (and inexpensive) methods of providing targeted leadership development training. Eighty-five percent of *Fortune* 500 corporations report using a multitude of learning platforms in the development of leaders. The most typical delivery methods include classroom training, web-based courses, and experiential learning activities (Orlando 2006).

  The leadership development tools selected for use in training are often stratified by leadership level. Classroom and e-learning tools are more prevalent for frontline and mid-level managers, whereas action learning techniques are most commonly targeted toward senior executives.

- **Executive sponsorship and active involvement:** As with any of the development initiatives outlined in this book, senior executive sponsorship and active involvement are essential to lending credibility to, and raising the organizational identity of, an in-house education and training program. In many companies, members of upper management are not only involved in the development and approval of the curricula and strategic learning plans, but also serve as faculty (representing their area of interest or expertise). At FedEx Corporation, every new supervisor or manager attends a series of leadership development courses facilitated by a senior-level executive. These courses focus on leadership values, competencies, and the organization's key initiatives. The executive team's significant time commitment to the program (two to three hours per class) demonstrates to participants that leadership development is a priority (Fulmer and Bleak 2007).

START FOCUSED, THEN EXPAND

Deciding how to start in-house training and development can be intimidating, particularly if your organization (as is typical in healthcare) has many pressing issues that could be the focus of educational strategies. Most successful organizations start slowly, focusing their educational efforts on one or two key strategic initiatives selected by the senior leadership team. This approach allows the facility's learning professionals to establish credibility and demonstrate how focused training advances the organization's strategic plans. Once curricula have been developed and delivered in response to these initial needs, a broader strategic learning plan can be implemented.

The leadership of Caterpillar Corporation, for example, created an internal learning function to boost progress toward its strategic goal of becoming a more efficient production operation. To improve productivity measurement processes, Caterpillar's learning professionals initially focused efforts on one key learning initiative: Six Sigma change management methodology training for every employee. After developing and delivering this curriculum, senior leadership created additional courses that focused on other company goals. Eventually, these courses were combined to create Caterpillar University, now one of the most respected corporate learning functions in the country (Vance 2008).

By starting small, focusing training on a few key business drivers, and creating early successes that add value to the organization, a successful in-house training program can be realized without placing undue stress on scarce financial and human resources.

REFERENCES

Field, A. 2004. "Corporate America's Learning Curve." *Fortune* (January): 31–36.

Fulmer, R., and J. Bleak. 2007. *The Leadership Advantage: How the Best Companies Are Developing Their Talent to Pave the Way for Future Success.* New York: AMACOM.

Orlando, C. 2006. "Leadership Development Practices of Top-Performing Organizations." [Online information; retrieved 10/13/08.] www.odl.rutgers.edu/e-leadership/pdf/Orlando.pdf.

Shell Oil. 2008. "Current Campaigns for Professionals." [Online information; retrieved 10/14/08.] www.shell.com/home/content/careers/current_campaigns/dir_current_campaigns.html.

Vance, D. 2008. "Learning Practices at Caterpillar, Lyceum to Wharton CLO Program." Seminar presented to chief learning officer program at the Wharton School of the University of Pennsylvania, Philadelphia, January 20.

Develop Depth Charts and Succession Plans for Key Positions

WHY FOCUS ON POSITIONS IN THE CONTEXT OF LEADERSHIP DEVELOPMENT?

Business pragmatism and the concern of governance board members are significant enough to require senior leadership to pay close attention to succession planning, especially related to positions at the top of the organization. The potential impact of a disaster, such as losing key leaders in an airplane crash, or something less sinister, such as routine turnover, should be addressed through position-related planning. For leaders at all levels, the value of smooth transitions is enormous.

In business books and articles on succession planning, the term *replacement planning* is typically used to refer to emergency succession planning that addresses the challenge of appointing replacements when vacancies in leadership positions have occurred in an ▶

unplanned or unexpected manner. In contrast, the term *succession planning* typically refers to a more orderly, structured process involving the identification and preparation of successors.

The term *succession planning* implies estimating the timing of anticipated position vacancies. An effective succession planning process should fill leadership openings as they are projected to occur. Organizations in the private sector have responded to the vacancy projection challenge in various ways, ranging from rough estimates of when openings are likely to occur (based primarily on relevant, anecdotal information) to complex mathematical models that predict attrition on the basis of extensive employee information, including historical patterns of hiring, promotion, and turnover. A classic article published in 1976 by the *Harvard Business Review* describes a detailed mathematical model called "managerial needs forecast," designed and used by Union Oil Company of California to calculate the number of leaders it will need at given points in time (Bright 1976). Armed with annual data provided by this model, the company's senior leaders turned their attention to the following questions:

- Who are the most promising leadership candidates?
- How ready are they for promotion?
- What are their development needs?
- What methods should be used to prepare these candidates in time?

Whether an organization uses an approach similar to this example or some other, less rigorous approach, the logic and challenge are basically the same: How much attrition is likely to occur in key positions, and how can employees with leadership potential be ready in time to fill these positions?

A RECOMMENDED EXERCISE TO ASSESS BENCH STRENGTH

For organizations with no formal succession planning process, and even those that have already implemented succession planning (but may not have developed the process completely), we suggest that senior leadership conduct the following demonstration project to assess the effectiveness of organizational succession planning initiatives.

- Designate a limited number of senior-level positions—at least the CEO position, its key direct reports, and, for larger organizations, a select number of other positions (for example, leaders of major hospitals/business units/corporate entities). For this exercise, the total number of positions should be manageable, ranging from about 6 to 12.

- List employees who possess the potential to fill each position, along with the following readiness designations:
  — Now
  — < 2 years
  — 2 to < 5 years
  — 5 to 10 years
  — > 10 years

  The list for each position should not be long. Why have 10 or 12 names on a depth chart if, for example, employees number 10, 11, and 12 will have a low probability of being assigned to the position when it becomes vacant?
- Assess the expected remaining tenure of each incumbent in the chosen positions.
- Summarize the results, placing special emphasis on employees who are expected to be ready by the incumbents' departure dates.
- Using your best business judgment, interpret the results of this exercise by assessing how confident your organization is that smooth transitions are likely when turnover is projected to happen in these positions.

This exercise will help measure the maturity of your succession planning and leadership development programs/efforts. The goal should be to identify candidates who are ready to assume key positions when they are expected to become vacant and are as capable as or more capable than the incumbents. This exercise may also serve to highlight key talent gaps that may need to be filled through external recruitment.

How Many Key Positions Should Be Selected for Succession Planning?

The answer to this question depends on the organization's definition of *key position*. The following illustration may be helpful in demonstrating some practical realities of depth chart development/succession planning.

Consider a hypothetical healthcare organization with 5,000 employees. Assume that its leadership positions are distributed as follows:

- Executives—15
- Level below executives (e.g., assistant or associate vice presidents, senior directors, directors)—85

- Managers (first- or second-level supervisors)—200
- Frontline supervisors (e.g., team leaders, shift leaders, supervisors in larger units)—200

In addition to the 500 formal leaders, 50 senior contributor positions exist that could be viewed as key due to the high level of technical/professional expertise required for successful performance of these roles and their importance to the organization.

Further assume that all 550 positions are considered key and that, ideally, depth chart development/succession planning should be applied to each. Let us examine how we might plan by category of leader.

EXECUTIVES Development of detailed depth charts/succession plans for each of the 15 executive positions is practical and meaningful. Some successors may appear on more than one of the 15 lists, possibly at different levels of readiness. If your organization does not have a formal succession planning initiative in place, development should begin with this group because although executives tend to be relatively few in number, they have the highest organizational impact.

ASSISTANT/ASSOCIATE VICE PRESIDENTS, SENIOR DIRECTORS, DIRECTORS Many of the 85 positions included in this category are likely to be sufficiently specialized to permit meaningful development of detailed depth charts/succession plans, resulting in unique lists of possible/planned successors. A number of these positions, however, will require the same or similar sets of leadership and functional competencies. Where overlap occurs, the recommended approach is to cluster these positions and refer to a single list of possible/planned successors applicable to this set. For example, an organization may choose to create a director category that comprises many positions, such as director of nursing, director of support services, and finance director, and develop cadres of individuals who would be potential successors to incumbents as attrition occurs. Rather than grooming a single nurse to be the director of a medical-surgical unit, the organization should focus on developing a larger number of individuals with the general leadership skills necessary to fill a variety of director roles, regardless of the specific patient care unit involved.

MANAGERS, FRONTLINE SUPERVISORS, AND SENIOR CONTRIBUTORS Some of these

450 positions (200 managers, 200 frontline supervisors, and 50 senior contributors) are likely to be sufficiently specialized to permit meaningful development of detailed depth charts/succession plans. Most, however, should be clustered into subgroups requiring the same or similar sets of leadership and functional competencies. As many lists of possible/planned successors should be developed as there are clusters of positions.

How to Assess Readiness

How does one interpret the concept of "ready now" to be assigned to a position? Does this status suggest a successor possesses all the leadership and functional competencies required by the new position? Half of them? Or a small percentage of them, along with a strong desire to be "stretched"?

We recommend that individuals be considered ready to assume a new position when they possess enough of the required competencies to perform the basic requirements of the position and have an opportunity to develop new or expanded competencies by working in it. In other words, the ideal successor (from an optimal development point of view) who is ready for a position will bring a lot of background and experience to the position and will gain new and improved competencies from aspects of the position that are totally or partially new.

Occasionally, however, business realities may demand that the ready successor bring a high percentage of relevant competencies to the new position, given the importance of the function to the business at that point in time. In these cases, the new position will present the successor with minimal development opportunities, but the time required to break in to the role will decrease, thus aiding the organization in the short term by having a fully productive incumbent sooner.

Avoid assigning an individual to a position that is foreign to his or her experiences and background or otherwise a poor match for existing competencies. Some senior leaders may view this type of assignment as evidence that the concepts of succession planning are fully embraced and the organization is willing to try unconventional assignments of talent. Generally speaking, these assignments fail; the organization and the individual will be damaged and nothing will be gained.

SUCCESSION PLANNING INFORMATION/DATA MANAGEMENT

Deciding to prepare a large number of quickly retrievable depth charts/succession plans is easy. Designing succession planning information management systems that will actually perform the function is harder. The good news is that software packages are available to assist with the considerable data collection, storage, and retrieval required to support an organization's succession planning processes (for example, work history/prior assignments, education record, licensure/certification record, employee preferences, and proposed future development steps). Review of all major alternatives is beyond the scope of this book, but considerable demand for these data systems has resulted in a number of quality choices in the marketplace. In the past, major private-sector companies developed their own proprietary software systems. This task is no longer necessary.

A CAUTIONARY NOTE ABOUT BUREAUCRACY

The suggestions in this book are not designed to burden the organization with unnecessary bureaucratic procedures and paperwork. Excessive bureaucratic procedures kill succession planning programs before they have a chance to prove their value. Paper forms and software systems should make relevant information management as easy as possible. Leadership oversight meetings should occur, but they should not take up an inordinate share of a leader's time. Employees and supervisors should devote sufficient time to crafting individualized development plans to foster employee growth, but such time should be well organized.

The ideas in this book require an increased time commitment from staff at all levels. We contend, and the experience of companies successful at leadership development show, however, that the advantages outweigh the investment.

REFERENCE

Bright, W. E. 1976. "How One Company Manages Its Human Resources." *Harvard Business Review* 54 (1): 81–93.

RECOMMENDED READING

Byham, W. C., A. B. Smith, and M. J. Paese. 2002. *Grow Your Own Leaders: How to Identify, Develop, and Retain Leadership Talent*. Upper Saddle River, NJ: Prentice-Hall Inc.

Faust, C. 2008. "Top 10 Steps to Managing Your Leadership Gap: The Impact of Effective Succession Planning." [Online information; retrieved 10/14/08.] www.softscape.com/whitepapers/nextgenleadersTM.htm.

Garman, A. N., and J. L. Tyler. 2004. "CEO Succession Planning in Freestanding U.S. Hospitals: Final Report." [Online information; retrieved 10/14/08.] www.ache.org/pubs/research/SuccessionRpt04.pdf.

NCHL and GE Institute for Transformational Leadership. 2008. "Preparing Leaders to Achieve Organizational Excellence." [Online information; retrieved 10/14/08.] www.nchl.org/ns/calendar/NCHL_Overview_1.08.pdf.

Provide Formal Oversight of the Leadership Development Process

HOW MUCH SENIOR LEADERSHIP OVERSIGHT OF DEVELOPMENT PROCESSES IS DESIRABLE?

At General Electric (GE), there is a significant infrastructure solely dedicated to the assessment and planned development of leaders. The most senior executives perform regular reviews of potential successors to the CEO position, and similar career potential reviews occur among leaders at all levels. This formal review and oversight allow GE to identify talented individuals early in their careers and develop them over the course of many years. The selection of Jack Welch as chairman and CEO in 1981 is a testament to the success of this focus on development. Welch was pulled from a pool of 96 qualified individuals, many of whom went on to run some of the largest companies in the nation after being passed over for the top post at GE (Slater 1993). ▶

Private companies with effective employee development processes oversee the process carefully. Decision-making authority is specifically and formally assigned to cascading levels of leadership. For example, at the top of the organization, a group comprising the CEO and specified direct reports may be assigned tasks such as

- evaluation and endorsement of career potential estimates for each individual currently in an executive position (particularly those below the levels represented in the decision-making group),
- approval of career advancement estimates for each individual with executive-level potential,
- assessment and approval of development plans for each individual currently at the executive level and for each individual with executive-level potential,
- approval of job rotations and reassignments for each individual currently at the executive level and for each individual with executive-level potential,
- approval of significant training/development experiences requiring expenditure of funds (e.g., university-based program, executive training program, on-

site leadership development course/academy, off-site training/development conference) for each individual currently at the executive level and each individual with executive-level potential,
- creation of depth charts for executive-level positions,
- establishment of new or revised executive positions,
- restructuring of significant segments of the organization, and
- adjudication of career development plans for all individuals who are part of a special program fostering high-potential talent streams (e.g., ex-administrative residents or fellows).

The CEO alone approves any action listed above that relates to a direct report.

WHAT IS THE PROPER OVERSIGHT ROLE OF LOWER-LEVEL LEADERSHIP?

Key operational units and functional groups, such as finance, patient care units, ancillary services, information technology, human resources, development (fundraising), and facilities management, oversee implementation of employee development processes. Leadership of these organizational units (normally a group led by an executive or a senior mid-level leader) may be assigned tasks complementary to those assigned to leaders at the top of the organization, such as

- establishment and endorsement of career potential estimates for each individual currently at manager level (normally second-level supervisors or above, or senior contributors at pay/position levels comparable to those of managers; executive levels not included);
- approval of career potential estimates for each individual with at least manager-level or equivalent contributor potential (but below the executive level);
- approval of development plans for each individual currently at manager level, or equivalent contributor level or above (but below the executive level) with comparable potential;
- approval of job reassignments for each individual currently at manager level, or equivalent contributor level or above (but below the executive level) with comparable potential;
- creation of depth charts for key positions below the executive level;

- establishment of manager-level positions and positions at an equivalent contributor level or above (but below the executive level);
- approval of unit restructuring within the broader organization (led by the decision-making group) (units smaller than the "significant segments of the organization" [applicable to the CEO and specified direct reports] referred to in the preceding section);
- approval of significant training/ development experiences requiring expenditure of funds for each individual currently at manager level, or equivalent individual contributor level or above (but below the executive level) with comparable potential; and
- advising the higher-level decision-making group on matters over which they have decision-making authority.

The lead executive of the business unit alone approves any action listed above that relates to a direct report.

For most organizations, a third level of leadership below the key operational unit or functional group level described above can be given decision-making authority over the lowest segment of employees (those currently at levels below manager level or equivalent contributor level). These decision-making groups are typically led by an individual at a level directly below executive level (e.g., assistant/associate vice president, senior director, director).

The reason for the cascade is to give authority to leaders closer to and more familiar with the performance and potential of the relevant groups of employees being evaluated. The suggestions listed above likely will need to be customized according to the specific structure of the organization. More complex, larger organizations may have a fourth level of oversight to reflect appropriate levels of leadership. The goal is to ensure that all levels of leadership are continually assessing their employees' potential and are working to develop these individuals in a structured and methodical fashion.

HOW FREQUENTLY SHOULD THESE GROUPS MEET TO PERFORM THEIR OVERSIGHT TASKS?

Meeting frequency will vary according to organizational need and complexity. Typically, oversight groups meet on a bimonthly, or even monthly, basis. Oversight groups for smaller organizational units may need to meet only on a quarterly basis. As processes become more familiar and recordkeeping and decision making become more efficient, meeting frequency may decrease.

WHAT ROLE SHOULD HUMAN RESOURCES PLAY IN FACILITATING THE LEADERSHIP DEVELOPMENT PROCESSES?

Although leaders at all levels should "own" the leadership development processes, human resources should be charged with providing expert support. This department may

- advise the design and continuous improvement of leadership development processes;
- consult with lead executive chairs and group members to schedule and plan oversight meetings and create agendas;
- attend these meetings, record decisions, and properly store this information;
- ensure that the decisions are implemented as planned, while facilitating the communication of decisions to the appropriate employees and key organizational stakeholders;

- conduct research/investigative projects and prepare development options and scenarios for key employees at the request of oversight group chairs or members; and
- draft forms and procedures for collecting and storing employee information relevant to the leadership development processes, including designing or selecting supporting software systems.

IS THERE AN EASIER WAY TO ACCOMPLISH THESE FUNCTIONS?

Unfortunately, there is no easier way to realize sustainable gain in leadership talent. Organizations in the private sector that are known for the quality of their leadership development processes report that their leadership groups spend significant, but not unreasonable, time implementing them. Decisions regarding career potential and appropriate succession planning for key positions are not easy to make and frequently require discussion and debate. Also, the thinking/analytical work required to prepare appropriate individual development plans is challenging and time consuming.

The willpower and discipline required to plan and implement key developmental job assignments are considerable. Unless an organization's leadership groups focus their efforts as described in the preceding sections, the employee development processes we have recommended will not be appropriately institutionalized and implemented on an ongoing basis. Simply challenging the organization to implement these processes without providing supporting systems and procedures will result in only short-term gains or outright failure. They will not happen systematically without formal leadership dedication.

REFERENCE

Slater, R. 1993. *The New GE: How Jack Welch Revived an American Institution.* Homewood, IL: Business One Irwin.

RECOMMENDED READING

Byham, W. C., A. B. Smith, and M. J. Paese. 2002. *Grow Your Own Leaders: How to Identify, Develop, and Retain Leadership Talent.* Upper Saddle River, NJ: Prentice-Hall Inc.

Collins, J., and J. Porras. 2004. *Built to Last: Successful Habits of Visionary Companies*. New York: HarperCollins.

McCall Jr., M. W. 1998. *High Flyers: Developing the Next Generation of Leaders*. Boston: Harvard Business School Press.

McCall Jr., M. W., and G. P. Hollenbeck. 2002. *Developing Global Executives: The Lessons of International Experience*. Boston: Harvard Business School Press.

Foster High-Potential Talent Streams

A CRITICAL QUESTION

Senior leaders in any industry question whether sufficient high-potential talent will emerge from disciplines traditionally recruited to fill mainstream positions. An organization has two strategic staffing choices: (1) depend on external recruiting for experienced resources with demonstrated leadership ability and/or (2) recruit specifically for leadership potential in addition to experience in key professional disciplines (e.g., marketing, engineering, finance, nursing, medical specialties, legal specialties).

Many healthcare recruiters have begun to seek individuals with administrative/managerial training. This trend has resulted in the proliferation of graduate programs in healthcare administration. Many organizations see these academic programs as suppliers of potential leaders who should be recruited as energetically as clinical professionals. Employer-sponsored ▶

programs offering tuition reimbursement encourage existing employees to seek advanced management degrees as a way to move up in the organization. Significant variations exist in the structure and rigor of these programs, however, and healthcare leaders that recruit talent from these academic institutions (or sponsor existing employees through degree plans) should know whether their healthcare management graduate programs are comprehensive.

MASTER'S PROGRAMS IN HEALTHCARE ADMINISTRATION

The names of master's programs in healthcare administration vary, but the most common degrees are

- Master of Business Administration: Health Sector Concentration (MBA),
- Master of Healthcare Administration (MHA),
- Master of Public Health (MPH), and
- Master of Health Services Administration (MHSA).

Similarities exist among these degrees. MBA programs tend to provide a general management core with additional courses in healthcare. MHA and MHSA programs tend to offer healthcare courses throughout the program, but usually offer some courses typically found in MBA programs (e.g., those with financial and organizational behavior emphases) with a healthcare orientation. MPH programs tend to resemble MHA and MHSA programs, but place more emphasis on the public sector.

What Do Master's Programs in Healthcare Administration Offer?

What knowledge and competencies can these programs impart to students? What skills differentiate graduates of these programs from employees without this specialized education?

Detailed information about the curricula of these programs, both on-line and campus-based, can be found at www.mastersinhealthcare.com. The following list describes some of the common areas/topics included in the curricula of schools featured on this website.

- **History of healthcare policy in the United States**
  — Overview of the organization, delivery, and financing of the U.S. healthcare system

— Social values; health policy, personnel, facilities, financing mechanisms, regulation, delivery models, quality assessment; program effects on patients, providers, and payers

■ **Economics of healthcare administration**
— Application of economic theory to healthcare, including supply and demand, elasticity, health insurance, regulation, competition, cost-effectiveness, and analysis for strategic planning

■ **Operations management in healthcare organizations**
— Applications of operations research techniques to healthcare planning, market analysis, decision making (including deterministic and random models)
— Mathematical programming, queuing, simulation forecasting, quality improvement, operating model formulation, outcome models based on potential operational decisions (scenarios)

■ **Healthcare organization theory**
— Formulation of organizational strategy; analysis of the impact of organization structure, individuals, groups, and environmental factors on organizational performance
— Case studies, concepts, leadership theory, research findings

in healthcare organizational behavior and administration

■ **Healthcare institutional management**
— Organization and management of modern healthcare institutions
— Major systems in organizations delivering healthcare services, including organizational design, governance, executive functions, clinical systems, support systems, communication theory, and interaction with external organizations

■ **Physicians and physician relationships**
— Introduction to the roles and responsibilities of physicians in the U.S. healthcare system
— Physician education, physician culture, practice patterns, physician leadership, management of physician practices, development of effective relationships between physicians and healthcare management

■ **Financial management for healthcare administration**
— Financial management concepts and techniques, differences between for-profit and not-for-profit organizations, regulatory constraints in the healthcare sector

- Managing working capital, analyzing and planning financial performance, cost of capital and capital budgeting, financial value and its determinants
- Forecasting future financial results, developing business plans
- Ratio analyses, cost accounting, rate setting, capital and operating budgeting, sources of financing, cash management, variance analysis, current financial issues

■ **Statistical analysis in healthcare organizations**
- Collection, aggregation, presentation of data; basic descriptive and inferential statistics
- Hands-on instruction in the application of spreadsheets and statistical software to the solution of various statistical problems

■ **Legal aspects of healthcare administration**
- Legal principles/processes influencing healthcare providers; basics of contract and tort law
- Major healthcare liability–producing areas and interface between law and ethics

■ **Human resources management in healthcare**
- Recruitment, selection, compensation, retention, and performance evaluation and management of healthcare resources
- Analysis of healthcare staffing issues; professional, technical, continuing education; credentialing; role of independent contractors of services
- Impact of federal legislation, such as National Labor Relations Act, Fair Labor Standards Act, Occupational Safety and Health Administration standards, equal employment opportunity laws, and Employee Retirement Income Security Act

■ **Information technology in healthcare**
- Electronic storage of healthcare information, data management systems, health information management; relationships with information technology vendors
- Regulatory issues in healthcare information technology
- Future of information technology in healthcare

■ **Health administration ethics**
- Case studies of ethical issues in healthcare
- Relationship between oversight of health institutions' moral mission and economic viability

■ **Current issues in healthcare**
- Study of contemporary issues in healthcare administration, including new forms of

organization for health services delivery, financing of healthcare, and increasing government regulation of health services

The success and proliferation of these master's programs in healthcare administration suggest that many organizations find value in recruiting graduates who understand these topics and have developed the competencies related to them.

Administrative Residencies and Fellowships

In addition to teaching the disciplines listed above, a majority of programs require an *administrative residency*—field experience in a healthcare organization under the supervision of a selected preceptor (or preceptors) and a university faculty member. Administrative residencies give students an opportunity to study how a healthcare organization functions in a variety of areas and gain practical experience.

To compete in today's flooded leadership market, many graduates of programs that do not require residencies seek a postgraduate fellowship in healthcare administration to make themselves more attractive to potential employers.

ROLE OF ADMINISTRATIVE RESIDENCIES AND FELLOWSHIPS The most successful companies have long recognized student internships and management trainee or fellowship-like programs for recent college graduates as effective ways of identifying and engaging new leadership talent. For example, Google Inc. (2008) allows college students to apply for internships in many of its key business functions, including online operations, finance, new business development, people operations (human resources), sales, and public affairs. This competitive program has produced a pipeline of young, talented individuals, supplying Google with a continuous stream of potential future leaders.

Like Google's program, fellowship and residency programs can create an ongoing source of leadership talent for healthcare organizations, particularly if long-term relationships are formed with top educational programs.

WHAT ARE THE KEY COMPONENTS OF AN ADMINISTRATIVE RESIDENCY OR A FELLOWSHIP? The purpose of a residency or fellowship is to develop graduates capable of assuming leadership positions in complex healthcare organizations. A residency or fellowship should focus on translating theoretical knowledge learned in the classroom into practical application.

Residencies and fellowships usually last 12 months, but duration may vary according to the sponsoring organization and the requirements of the educational institution. The most successful programs consist of two broad components or phases that occur simultaneously.

I. **Orientation/rotation phase—** During this phase, the resident/ fellow participates in a comprehensive orientation. The goal is for the resident/fellow to become familiar with the sponsoring organization's structure, strategic plans, system initiatives, core businesses and services, and administrative leadership team. This phase typically consists of rotational experiences in areas such as operations/patient care, corporate services, legal, finance, and human resources, which are intended to provide a broad knowledge of all areas in the organization.

II. **Implementation/performance phase—**During this phase, a preceptor assigns projects to the resident/fellow that are designed to provide a rich learning opportunity as well as benefit the sponsoring organization. Upon completion of each project, the resident/fellow and the preceptor discuss and evaluate the impact it had on the resident/fellow and its implications for the organization. These assignments give the resident/fellow an opportunity to apply knowledge gained through didactic training and to develop his or her ability to engage in critical thinking, analysis, and problem solving in a variety of settings.

LEADERSHIP ENGAGEMENT IN RESIDENCY OR FELLOWSHIP EXPERIENCES Sponsoring a residency or fellowship program in healthcare administration can be an excellent means of attracting new talent to an organization, but it requires significant engagement at all levels of leadership and can be time consuming (particularly for the program's primary preceptors). The primary preceptor should be a high-level executive in the organization to lend credibility to the program, identify and assign projects of strategic importance, and facilitate the rotational experiences critical to the student's development. In exchange for this significant commitment of time and energy, the sponsoring organization can have 12-month "working interviews" with talented, degreed candidates who could significantly raise the skill level of middle management as they transition into their first work assignments.

FORMALLY MANAGING THE EARLY CAREERS OF EMERGING LEADERS

Managing the career paths of young, emerging leaders poses many opportunities and challenges. If these motivated individuals do not feel that the organization is paying close attention to their ongoing success, they will quickly disengage and may be lured away by another organization. The significant investment of time and energy placed into growing the skill sets of these individuals will have been for naught, and a competing organization will realize the benefits of these labors.

In an attempt to retain top young talent, many companies have created formal programs designed to handpick work assignments for the first two to three years of these individuals' careers. AT&T, for example, established a leadership development program in 1988 with a goal of growing and retaining emerging leaders. The program targets new employees who are recent MBA graduates and demonstrate the skills necessary to perform well in various leadership positions across the company. Participants are placed in three diverse work assignments over 24 to 28 months, including two supervisory roles (typically in challenging union environments). AT&T has realized a significant reduction in turnover of mid-level leaders since the advent of the program and has created a pipeline of leaders who possess leadership skills that are translatable to a variety of work settings (AT&T 2008).

This same level of attention should be placed on managing the early careers of high-potential employees in healthcare organizations, particularly those who have completed an administrative residency or fellowship. We would suggest that, at a minimum, the first three work assignments of those with the highest potential should be carefully planned and "owned" by senior leadership. In keeping with the model demonstrated by AT&T, the experiences should be diverse (e.g., operations/patient care, finance, planning), roughly 12 to 15 months in length, and designed to provide a broad knowledge base that will prepare these individuals to assume key leadership roles. This type of rotational approach to an early career path is not common in healthcare. The highest levels of leadership must support transitional learning and manage pushback from business units that have invested in an employee for 12 to 15 months when the employee moves on to the next assignment. Formalization and communication of an early careerist program (such as AT&T's leadership development program) not only demonstrates organizational (rather than departmental) ownership of the career paths of emerging leaders, but also can help set the expectations of program participants and those who will guide and supervise them.

REFERENCES

AT&T. 2008. "Careers: Leadership Development Program." [Online information; retrieved 10/14/08.] www.att.com/gen/careers?pid=12.

Google Inc. 2008. "Building Opportunities for Leadership & Development (BOLD): Google's Diversity Internship Program. [Online information; retrieved 10/14/08.] http://google.com/support/jobs/bin/static.py?page=bold.html.

RECOMMENDED READING

"Masters in Health Care." www.mastersinhealthcare.com.

Epilogue

The Future of Leadership Development in Healthcare

PREDICTED TRENDS

Where do we believe leadership development is headed in healthcare? The trend descriptions on the following page represent our best predictions, challenges, and hopes for the future. We chose to label two columns "From" and "To" versus "Current State" and "Future State" or "Past Practice" versus "Best Practice" because a number of more progressive organizations may already be demonstrating the behaviors listed in the right-hand column. Also, we believe labeling these practices as best practices is risky and a bit presumptuous because the term is relative and, hopefully, temporary. Today's best practices may appear limited or primitive to those who look at them from the vantage point of the future. ▶

From	To
Leadership Development Process Parsimony	
Multiple processes throughout the organization; processes delegated to each division/large unit; inability to explain to employees how processes typically work in the broader organization	Common processes used throughout the organization; compelling, motivating story to tell employees regarding consistency, quality, and outcomes of processes
Ownership of Development Processes	
Employee ownership of individual development; job posting is most important process; career paths largely unplanned by leaders	Shared ownership of career development and related processes; career paths systematically planned according to a variety of information, including employee interests and ongoing assessment of competency gaps
Involvement/Sponsorship of Senior Leaders	
Lip service by, but minimal commitment of, leaders at all levels; little sponsorship from top management	High commitment of leaders at all levels; leaders' personal success correlated with effectiveness in this area
Career Employment	
Assumption that leadership vacancies must be filled by external candidates; career development is not a core organizational value	Expectation that a high percentage of leadership vacancies will be filled through promotion from within; career development is a core organizational value
Development Methods	
Emphasis on classroom training and self-study; lack of internal development process prompts employees to employer hop at strategic times in their careers to meet individual goals	Focus on gaining challenging experiences from on-the-job activity, such as job rotation, interim assignments, and special projects, all for the purpose of career development
Staff Support	
Limited or no qualified staff to support employee development processes	Sufficient human resources staff to guide and support processes
Identification of High-Potential Resources	
No formal processes related to early identification of high-potential resources	Formal annual career potential estimates, supported by in-depth knowledge of employees' competencies, resulting in early and ongoing identification of high-potential resources

(continued)

Focus of Succession Planning	
A few select high-potential resources slated to fill top positions	Many pools of high-potential employees groomed to fill a variety of key positions
Personnel/Career Information	
Nonexistent or severely limited employee data supporting development processes	Readily available employee data in areas such as job assignment history, career interests, competency gaps, individual development plans, and key position plans
Early Career Experiences	
No systematic focus on planning early career experiences	Focus on early career experiences involving risk taking to accelerate development and validate estimates of potential
Leadership Decision-Making Structure	
No formalized leadership review of development issues	Formal leadership meetings/review of development issues, assigned according to authority delegation guides in a cascading fashion from senior to lower levels
Continuous Process Improvement	
Process outcomes not measured or tracked; process improvement not rigorous or systematic	Process outcomes measured and evaluated; continuous improvement approach results in increasingly effective processes

WHERE DOES YOUR ORGANIZATION STAND?

An objective assessment of the state of your organization in reference to the 12 continua above may be sobering. Making progress in these areas is likely to be challenging, not only because the work outlined in this book can be difficult, but also because cultural change of this magnitude can be daunting. However, study of the for-profit, big-business world indicates enormous benefits can be realized by organizations that are able to make substantial progress in implementing these processes, especially in the following areas:

- Greater retention of high-potential human resources
- Faster and more targeted development of resources, especially those with high potential

- Smoother transitions when key leadership vacancies are filled
- Greater commitment of rank-and-file employees, because they realize the organization cares about them and their careers enough to engage in formal career planning

HOW DO WE MEASURE THE SUCCESS OF LEADERSHIP DEVELOPMENT ACTIVITIES?

Leadership development activities will be supported to the extent they make a critical strategic or economic difference. Without evidence of significant added value, there is little chance of keeping the interest, involvement, and ongoing support of senior leadership, especially when priorities are competing for time and resources. Linking formal leadership development initiatives to improved outcomes is a difficult task because many forces, not only leadership development, affect success. Even companies with mature development systems struggle with quantifying the benefit of their initiatives. Although difficult, demonstrating the impact of leadership development is not impossible, and evaluation methods should be considered before implementing

the lessons outlined in this book. A proven evaluation framework should be incorporated into the design of the development programs. Donald Kirkpatrick and James Kirkpatrick (2006), in their book *Evaluating Training Programs*, created a four-level method of categorizing evaluation data that has been used extensively to isolate the impact of learning and development initiatives. We recommend using this framework for program evaluation.

Four-Level Evaluation Framework

Level 1: Evaluating Reaction

Level 2: Evaluating Learning

Level 3: Evaluating Behavior

Level 4: Evaluating Results

Level 1: Evaluating Reaction: Assessing Participants' Initial Reaction to the Initiatives to Determine Their Satisfaction

These data are typically gathered by providing an evaluation survey to program participants. The survey allows individuals to provide feedback on areas of the program (e.g., formal mentoring, classroom-based learning activities, rotational job assignments) they felt provided the greatest value and on program components they would change.

Level 2: Evaluating Learning: Determining Whether Participants Learned the Key Concepts of the Initiatives

What knowledge and skills have participants acquired as a result of the initiatives? The easiest and most cost-effective method of determining whether a participant has retained key concepts is to create a questionnaire that highlights his or her focus areas. For example, if the participant's development plan focused on improving communication skills, an appropriate question might be: *How would you describe your ability to communicate information in a clear and specific manner?* The organization may choose to keep these surveys quantitative and have respondents rate their abilities on a five-point scale, from very good communication ability to very poor, or it may choose to use open-ended survey questions and have respondents describe how the program has helped them improve their communication skills.

Level 3: Evaluating Behavior: Measuring Change in Participants' Behavior Since Implementation of Leadership Development Initiatives

How has the program affected on-the-job performance? This level of evaluation typically involves information gathered not from the individual being developed, but from those with whom he or she frequently interacts. A source of data might be a survey sent to the employee's direct supervisor, asking him or her to rate the employee's performance, or data might be extracted from the employee's performance reviews to determine whether program participation has brought about an appreciable change in the employee's behavior. Some organizations with mature leadership development systems gather feedback not only from the employee's supervisor, but also from peers, subordinates, and customers.

Level 4: Evaluating Results: Determining the Initiatives' Impact on the Success of the Organization

The goal of leadership development programs is to advance the organization toward its strategic goals. Stephen Covey (1989), in his book *Seven Habits of Highly Effective People*, says to begin with the end in mind and allow the goals to drive the focus of development efforts. To demonstrate that these initiatives have contributed to the overall success of the organization, we recommend choosing key metrics that will be evaluated in individuals who are the focus of development activities. For example, a balanced scorecard approach could include the following metrics in the employee's area of responsibility: staff turnover rates, financial performance relative to budget, employee satisfaction, patient satisfaction, regulatory compliance, and a host of other critical options. These measures should be objective and linked to the overall goals of the organization.

DEMONSTRATING A RETURN ON INVESTMENT FROM LEADERSHIP DEVELOPMENT

Because of the significant investment of time and resources required to successfully implement a structured leadership development program, many organizations have attempted to quantify their return on investment (ROI). Calculating ROI from development and training activities is not as simple as evaluating the payback period for a new MRI scanner; estimations and assumptions must be made. With appropriate structure and diligence, however, calculations can be made that will be well received by even the most stalwart chief financial officer.

Assume, for example, that a hospital invested $15,000 in training the director of radiology in Six Sigma as part of her professional development plan. One year after the training, staff productivity in radiology improved so much that the organization realized $200,000 in additional revenues. The critical question is: How much of this improvement can be attributed to the training? The answer can be obtained by asking the director of radiology the following questions:

- What percentage of this improvement would you attribute to the concepts you learned in the Six Sigma training course?
- What is the basis for your estimation?
- What other factors may have contributed to this improvement?

The success of this approach relies on the assumption that the director of radiology can accurately estimate how much of the improvement relates to her training. A study published in 2003 by leadership and training author Jack Phillips revealed that in instances where performance improved, participants were able to make surprisingly accurate estimates of the impact of their training and development on the realized gains, using the questions outlined above. He went on to propose the following calculation for determining ROI of development activities:

$$\text{ROI (\%)} = \text{Net program benefits} / \text{Program costs} \times 100$$

Assume that the radiology director attributes 75 percent of the realized gains to the implementation of Six Sigma methodology. The ROI calculation for the training investment would be:

$$\text{ROI (\%)} = \text{Increased productivity (\$200,000)} \times \% \text{ attributed to training (0.75)} / \text{Program costs (\$15,000)} \times 100$$

$$\text{ROI} = 1,000\%$$

Obviously, the example provided above is simplistic and focuses on only one training program rather than a series of development activities, but it does illustrate that numerical estimations of return can be made.

FINAL THOUGHTS

Best-practice organizations recognize that relying on a series of unrelated training programs is not nearly as effective as designing an integrated leadership development system through which high-potential individuals are exposed to a variety of experiences linked by an overarching strategy. This developmental strategy should be driven by your organization's strategic goals and defined by your leadership values and competencies. Leadership at the highest levels must endorse and participate in the formal development initiatives to lend credibility to the efforts.

As practicing healthcare administrators, the authors understand that the prospect of implementing the concepts outlined in this book may be daunting, particularly if little or no leadership development infrastructure exists in your organization. We advise anyone seeking to establish or improve their organization's development activities to remember that leadership development is a journey and not an event, and every journey begins with a first step.

REFERENCES

Covey, S. 1989. *Seven Habits of Highly Effective People*. New York: Fireside.

Kirkpatrick, D., and J. Kirkpatrick. 2006. *Evaluating Training Programs: The Four Levels*, 3rd edition. San Francisco: Berrett-Koehler Publishers, Inc.

Phillips, J. 2003. *Return on Investment in Training and Performance Improvement Programs*, 2nd edition. Boston: Butterworth-Heinemenn Publishers, Inc.

ABOUT THE AUTHORS

Brett D. Lee, PhD, FACHE, currently serves as a vice president at Children's Medical Center–Dallas, where he oversees clinical and family support departments. In addition to his operational responsibilities, he pursues his passion of implementing effective leadership development systems in healthcare organizations. Dr. Lee is a faculty member of the internal leadership academies for directors and managers at Children's, and a preceptor and coordinator of students completing their administrative residencies at the center.

Dr. Lee remains active as an academic, publishing frequently and serving on the adjunct faculty of the Johns Hopkins School of Public Health. He is a former member of the inaugural cohort of students in the executive program in work-based learning leadership at the prestigious Wharton School at the University of Pennsylvania, where he studied leadership development alongside top chief learning officers.

James W. Herring, PhD, is senior vice president, administration, at Children's Medical Center–Dallas, where he is responsible for law, human resources, governance, compliance, and internal audit, and works to incorporate superior practices from general industry into the center's preeminent leadership development program. Prior to Children's, he spent much of his time designing and implementing leadership development and succession planning systems. His career spans almost 40 years, including over 20 years as a human resources professional (mostly at executive level) at Exxon Mobil Corporation and 15 years as a consultant to large private-sector and government organizations.

Dr. Herring remains active as an academic, having current or past adjunct faculty and intern/resident preceptor affiliations with five universities—Johns Hopkins University (School of Public Health), University of Houston (Psychology Department), The University of Texas at Arlington (Psychology Department), University of Dallas (School of Management), and Houston Baptist University (College of Business and Economics).